D0974978

JOHN KRAMP

on TRACK

*L*EADERSHIP

{ MASTERING WHAT LEADERS ACTUALLY DO }

BROADMAN
&HOLMAN
PUBLISHERS

NASHVILLE, TENNESSEE

Ten-Digit ISBN: 0–8054–4018–4
Thirteen-Digit ISBN: 978–0–8054–4018–8

Published by Broadman & Holman Publishers
Nashville, Tennessee

Dewey Decimal Classification: 303.3
Subject Heading: LEADERSHIP

Scripture quotations are taken from the Holman Christian
Standard Bible® Copyright © 1999, 2000, 2002, 2004 by
Holman Bible Publishers. Used by permission.

1 2 3 4 5 6 7 8 9 10   10 09 08 07 06

To Pastor Scott Patty
and the people of Grace Community Church
Brentwood, Tennessee

Contents

Prologue

IN THE LATE NINETIES, I ATTENDED THE KELLOGG SCHOOL of Management in Chicago and completed an MBA. For twenty years before that, I lived life in the context of local church ministry. As a result, I was curious (and intimidated) by what I would face at one of the finest business schools in the country. What I discovered, though, surprised me. Boiled down to its essence, Kellogg gave me two things: leadership models and leadership tools.

Leadership Models

The professors at Kellogg loved case studies. Initially, such cases stumped me. I couldn't understand the benefit of dissecting the story of, for example, a tool-and-dye plant in the 1960s. What I discovered was that these case studies presented real-life examples of real leaders running real businesses facing real problems. They revealed timely and timeless models of leadership that fit current-day problems perfectly. The case studies gave us models for leadership, for how to think about business and how to solve business problems.

Leadership Tools

In addition to giving us business models, the professors at Kellogg sought to give us business tools. They talked about loading up our "toolboxes" with a full set of tools we would need to face a changing set of business challenges. They wanted us to have tools and know how to use them.

Models and tools—that's what Kellogg gave me. But Kellogg gave me something else, something unintentional. Kellogg helped me to see and value the models and tools I already had from years in ministry.

A Personal Case Study

I began to think about the five years I spent starting a new church in Portland, Oregon. That intense experience became a case study which offered a model for leadership. That experience highlighted the tools needed for effective leadership and forced me to improve in my ability to use those skills.

For a long time I thought the only case studies that would help other people were success stories. My church-planting experience was far from such a story. But it is a good story—a story of risk and reward, of attempts and failures, of progress and setbacks, of exhilaration and discouragement. Looking back on it with more than a decade of perspective, I now believe my experience can at least serve as a useful case study. From the case study emerges a model of leadership. The model highlights the essential skills required for leadership. My mistakes and missteps along the way should make the case study more believable and certainly less intimidating.

I learned much about leadership by reflecting on my experience in starting a new church. That reflection led to the *On-Track Leadership* model. My hope is that this simple model will help you understand the whole and the parts of leadership so that you can lead with increasing effectiveness.

All you have to do to get started is to remember this: leadership is like a train.

The Leadership Train Introduction

LEADERSHIP IS LIKE A TRAIN.

Imagine you're driving your car down the interstate, parallel to a train chugging along the track. You notice the train with little awareness of the individual cars. Now imagine that same train as it cuts through your town. Guardrails block you for seventeen minutes at a crossing three blocks from your home. Your perspective changes. You now analyze the train car by car. You study its engine, passenger cars, fuel cars, equipment cars, and caboose.

Most of us view leaders like trains along the interstate. We notice them. We may say, "There's a leader." Most of the time, however, we pay little attention to a leader's specific actions. The situation changes when we must lead. Now we view leadership like a train at a railroad crossing. We focus on the individual actions in the process we call leadership. We analyze the actions and seek to understand how they stand alone and fit together.

Let's stop at the crossing and analyze a Leadership Train. The Leadership Train includes five cars:

1. The Engine—vision and personal planning
2. The Passenger Car—enlisting and team building
3. The Fuel Car—communication and delegation
4. The Equipment Car—motivation and correction
5. The Caboose—celebration

The Engine in the Leadership Train

This engine combines two parts of leadership: vision and personal planning.

Vision pulls the leadership process. The stronger the vision, the more it can pull. Without vision the other cars on the Leadership Train stand still.

Vision asks leaders, "What do you see?" To answer that question, leaders identify needs unmet, hurts unhealed, and tasks undone. Through visioning, they see the gaps between what is and what could be. Slowly leaders focus what they see. Pictures emerge. Ideas develop. Vision grows.

As engines require engineers, so vision requires personal planning to direct it, to channel its potential power. Personal planning acts as another level of visioning. The leader asks the question, "How do I get to what I see?" To answer this question leaders hone their vision. They identify where they are, where they want to be, and possible routes to get there. Leaders set the overall direction required to reach the vision.

The Passenger Car in the Leadership Train

Leaders add followers like engines add cars. In this Leadership Train, we add the passenger car by combining two parts of leadership: (1) enlisting, and (2) team building.

Leaders cannot reach envisioned destinations alone. So leaders enlist others to make the trip with them, not as passengers only but as fellow workers on the train. Enlisting asks people, "Would you like to go there with me?" Through vision and personal planning, leaders already set the specific destination and general direction of the Leadership Train. This knowledge enables the leader to say when enlisting, "I'm going; do you want to come?"

At this point the leader faces danger. The passenger car may fill with sightseers rather than workers. Sightseers add weight to the train without providing work. They hinder the journey to the vision. Through team building, wise leaders add workers rather than sightseers. Team building asks the question, "How should we get there?" Leaders care about the vision, the final destination, and the direction. They leave room, however, for the workers in the passenger car to shape the route the train will travel. As the workers forge the direction and make group plans, team spirit grows. More important, *the* vision becomes *our* vision.

The Fuel Car in the Leadership Train

The journey toward the vision destination drains the energy of the engine. The third car in this Leadership Train is the fuel car. This car adds two additional parts of leadership: (1) communication, and (2) delegation. Together they keep the fuel level high.

Communication builds on the work completed by team building. Team building, with its focus on group planning, sparks insights. The group gains understanding of the destination and the journey. Individuals learn the perspectives of their team members.

Communication responds by asking this question: "What do we see?" Process becomes priority at this stage in visioning. The leader and the team work to state their vision in concise language complete with measurable goals. This process requires listening, understanding, stating (and restating!) ideas. Leaders guide the group toward a mission statement that describes the team's new understanding of its vision and plan.

Communication makes delegation possible. Delegation asks the question: "Which part of our plan is your responsibility?" If team members have personally shaped the plan, they will gladly work in areas where they can make the greatest contribution. The leader guides team members to determine spiritual gifts, temperament, talents, and values. The leader then helps ensure that team members do work that uses their strengths. If anyone shirks responsibility for part of the plan, the leader knows that person is a sightseer and not a worker. This is the ideal place to suggest that such a person get off the train!

The Equipment Car in the Leadership Train

A wise leader plans for adjustments along the way to the vision. To accomplish this the Leadership Train adds its fourth car, the equipment car, with two additional parts of leadership: (1) motivation, and (2) correction.

Motivation asks the question: "Are we still moving toward our goal?" Wise leaders recognize that people motivate themselves. Internal motivation occurs when people move toward a vision they value, follow plans they help develop, and work in their areas of strength. Leaders seek to remove obstacles to internal motivation like fatigue and distraction. Leaders remind the team of the facts: this is our vision and our plan; we need each of you to reach our destination.

Correction asks the question: "I think we're off target. Do you?" Leaders recognize the tendency for teams to lose sight of their vision and stray from their plans. Correction seeks positive options. The leader simply says, "We're not reaching the goals we set. Do we need to reevaluate our plan? Or do we simply need to adjust and move again in the direction we set?" Leaders constantly watch the direction of the team, checking the current course against the vision destination.

The Caboose in the Leadership Train

The final car on the Leadership Train is the caboose of celebration. Celebration says, "Wow! That's great!" Wise leaders know that teams need celebration throughout the trip toward the vision destination. Celebrating the small successes along the way reinforces every part of the leadership process. Leaders notice someone doing something that embodies the values and commitment required to reach the vision. Even if the action is small, the leader celebrates. As the team passes through strategic points along the journey, the leader encourages celebrations of progress. Celebration is more than motivation. Celebration undergirds the values that fuel motivations. Good leaders celebrate the end of the journey. Wise leaders celebrate throughout the journey.

The model for the Leadership Train flows from my experience in beginning a new church. Here's how I worked through each stage of leadership in this ministry:

1. Visioning—In February 1987 I sensed God calling me to plant a new church in a suburb of Portland, Oregon, called Lake Oswego. Through observation and study I learned all I could about the area. I searched for existing needs. A church effectively reaching secular adults for Christ and helping them grow spiritually emerged as the strategic need. Planting that kind of church became my vision destination.

2. Personal Planning—For six months I learned all I could about starting mission churches, especially on the West Coast. Based on what I learned, I set the general direction we would follow to begin Westside Baptist Church. The final vision remained somewhat fuzzy for me. I could, however, see the vision clearly enough to get moving. With these two steps in place, I had my engine for this Leadership Train.

3. Enlisting—My vision far exceeded what I could do by myself. The first year of the life of Westside centered on enlisting people who glimpsed my vision for this new church. I shared my vision with two men who joined me as associate pastors. I shared the vision with people who visited our Sunday worship service. Slowly a group emerged who said they wanted to help fulfill the vision.

4. Team Building—Early on I underestimated how much I needed the group planning part of the leadership process. Initially I carried the full burden as "keeper of the vision." In time I learned that God was sending team members who would work with me to understand and pursue the vision. I helped them see the vision that brought me to Oregon. They helped me see the vision with greater clarity.

I sensed the Leadership Train now had an engine and a passenger car.

5. Communication—We struggled throughout the second year of our church's history to communicate our mission with clarity. Finally, we settled on this statement: "Westside is a church learning to love God and love people with creativity, passion, and joy." It was not a perfect statement, but it was ours, and we began to build on it.

6. Delegation—Our team members grew in our understanding of our mission and of one another's gifts. We helped people find the place where they could serve with creativity, passion, and joy. At this stage we faced the realization that our passenger car included far more sightseers than expected. At least we had connected our fuel car to our engine and passenger car.

7. Motivation—I learned along the way that if people believe we are pursuing the right vision, using the right plan (usually one they helped develop), and are providing a way for them to serve with satisfaction, they generate their own motivation. I helped people find a place on the team where they could demonstrate their love for God and other people. Of course we struggled to fill positions for which no one showed passion, much less creativity and joy.

8. Correction—Leadership demanded I keep the team moving toward the vision destination. Confusion dogged me. Many times I felt lost. In those times I called the team together, and we looked at the vision and adjusted our course to correct any deviation. Along the way a few people decided they no longer wanted to pursue our vision and stepped off the train. Fortunately, they did so without damaging the train or impeding our progress.

9. *Celebration*—I learned much about the art of finding excuses to celebrate. Church anniversaries became treasured times for us. I learned to create personal celebrations by affirming individuals doing their work as part of our team. I sensed that celebration enhanced every part of the leadership process.

We grow as leaders while we attempt to lead. You can lead. You just need to start slowly and link your personal Leadership Train. Start with an engine—vision and planning. Move toward what you see. You'll be amazed. Head out of the station, and people will climb aboard.

....

Vision: "What Do I See?"

....

A LEADER SEES THINGS . . . THINGS THAT DON'T EXIST. WHAT leaders see that others don't see motivates people to follow them. I am using *visioning* for the ability to see what Paul referred to in 2 Corinthians 4:18 as things that are unseen. *Visioning* for a business leader might be the ability to see markets and strategies for economic growth. *Visioning* for a Christian leader is seeing spiritual realities, spiritual goals, and spiritual strategies. Visioning may be a part of a businessman's ability, but *spiritual* visioning is an ability possible only for Christians. Henry Blackaby talks about this kind of visioning when he encourages Christians to find out where God is at work and join Him. Vision is the engine that pulls the Leadership Train.

Vision continues as a hot topic in business and in the church. Everyone wants a vision. Yet confusion reigns. Vision remains elusive. Most who want vision cannot convince themselves they have it.

Vision awes many Christians. It looms grand, mysterious, the property of super-spiritual saints who tackle great tasks for God. Persons perceived to have vision sometimes seem to be a special breed that God rewards with crystal-clear mental pictures of the future. Awed by vision, some Christians believe it is not standard equipment for everyday Christians.

We cannot allow vision to awe us, nor can we make vision the exclusive property of a spiritual elite. Somehow vision should become standard equipment for all Christians.

Biblical Snapshots of Visioning

The Bible provides ample examples of everyday people developing vision and acting on that vision.

Four visioning friends brought a lame man to Jesus. Long before they saw Jesus, they saw their friend lying before Him. They saw, in their vision, Jesus touch their friend, heal their friend. That vision—a picture that existed initially only in their minds—drove them to act. They persisted. They overcame obstacles. Finally, a group of people and even Jesus saw the four lower their friend to the floor from a rough-cut hole in the roof. When Jesus healed that man, the crowd saw the fulfillment of a vision.

Another day Jesus fed more than five thousand people from a little lad's lunch. A major-league miracle, we say. And yet, didn't it begin with a minor-league vision? A little unnamed boy and Andrew, an astute disciple, saw something others didn't see. They saw a three-way connection between a boy's sack lunch, a hungry crowd, and Jesus. Jesus acted on what they saw. He multiplied that boy's fish and bread into a sit-down dinner for more than five thousand. The crowd saw the fulfillment of a vision.

The Question Many Must Ask

The Bible shows us that vision belongs in the public domain. Until Christians understand and assume their rightful role as visionaries, our churches, our ministries will suffer. There can be no spiritual progress without leadership. There can be no leadership without vision.

Vision begins when you answer this question: What do I see? When you look beyond a situation as it is and picture what could be (ta-da!), you have vision.

"But," you say, "I don't see anything big. I can't call what I see a vision!" Don't worry. Most people with vision don't see "big things." More often they simply see a small gap where life could be better, usually in a neglected area overlooked by others. That gap becomes their vision, their opportunity for leadership.

A member of First Church Somewhere notices several young couples in her church who are new Christians. She knows that without help they will never grow as Christians. They will not mature spiritually or serve effectively.

Aha! She has identified a gap, something that *is* pointing toward something that *could be.* A vision develops in her mind. She sees a group of people meeting each week. She sees them sitting together, talking, laughing, sharing. In her mind she can hear them asking questions about how to grow as a Christian. She pictures a leader guiding the group through materials that help them develop their spiritual lives. She imagines the group growing. She enjoys the thought of these people becoming effective leaders in the church.

None of what she sees exists except in her mind. Yet there in her vision it exists. The mental picture, her vision, is the first step of leadership, the engine that will pull her Leadership Train.

Until something exists in a vision, it will not exist in reality. Vision always precedes reality. When we see reality, we see the substance and fulfillment of someone's vision.

Where do these visions come from? Does God give them? Do we create them? The distinction is important. If God gives the vision, our role is a passive receiver. If vision germinates in our heart and grows, our role is more active. So is vision passive or active?

The Bible doesn't address this issue specifically. Certainly Scripture provides ample examples of people with vision. It doesn't, however, tell us the source of their vision.

The Classic Picture of Visioning

Nehemiah is the classic model to consider as we seek to answer this question. Christian books on vision often feature Nehemiah. This prophet envisioned a wall around Jerusalem even though he had never been there. Nonetheless, in his mind he saw a wall. Jerusalem's wall became his vision. His vision became the first step in that wall becoming a reality.

Did God give Nehemiah that vision? The Bible doesn't say. We do know that Nehemiah had an intimate relationship with God. He developed values and interests that spawned a vision for a wall. God used Nehemiah's vision. In the end a wall existed for all to see.

Did Nehemiah wait to receive a vision from God? Was he searching for something to do with his life? Did he long for a task with eternal significance, a breathtaking undertaking?

I believe that Nehemiah's vision bubbled up from the normal course of his life and walk with God. God obviously could have, but didn't need to etch "The Wall Vision" on Nehemiah's heart. God did something even more amazing. God found a man whose situation and values, spiritual passion, and personal drive caused him to care about

Jerusalem's habitation and protection. Then on God's schedule He ensured that Nehemiah got the news that Jerusalem needed a new wall—and needed it now! Instant connection: Jerusalem's missing wall and Nehemiah's passionate concern fused into a vision. God blessed that vision.

The Role of Vision in Leadership

Do you have a vision? Look for needs you care about. Look for wrong that needs to be made right. Look for a needed ministry that doesn't exist. In these gaps you may find your vision.

Perhaps your mental pictures aren't so clear. Many people feel that fuzzy vision means no vision. Vision by nature appears fuzzy. Vision is the starting point. Vision needs the other cars in the Leadership Train such as planning, communication, enlisting, and team building. Additional elements fine-tune vision. Don't expect vision to be clearer than it can be.

Vision is like the engine of a train. It gets things moving. Vision says, "All aboard. We're leaving." Others hook on. Until vision moves, nothing happens.

A Personal Case Study in Vision

On March 13, 1988, I saw one vision in my life become reality. On that Sunday morning in a high school gymnasium, our mission church in Lake Oswego, Oregon, had its first service with more than two hundred people in attendance. That morning culminated a year of work by more than five hundred families from our sponsor church, the First Baptist Church of Garland, Texas. Months earlier those wonderful people glimpsed what I did, a new church in a growing suburb of Portland. Based on that vision, they made more than forty-three thousand long-distance phone calls from Texas to Oregon inviting people to attend our first service. They even paid their own phone bills! Now that's commitment.

I confess that during the months of planning and work that led up to our first service, I worried about the quality of my vision. There were times when I couldn't see the future clearly. Many days my fears clouded what little I could see.

Some Christian leaders move as if God has etched the future for them in 3–D. My vision was more like watching an old black-and-white garage sale television complete with floppy rabbit ears, fuzz, blips, and rolling lines. I wanted to see the future more clearly. I wanted God to drop a large-screen, color-enhanced, high-definition vision into my mind. But if God was beaming me a high-definition signal, my antenna didn't receive it.

All I had was a strong desire to begin a new church. I sensed God had led me to move two thousand miles from my family and friends; so my wife and our two young daughters moved. I wrote a plan for how I would begin a new church in a tough area. At the time that plan was all I knew to do.

Looking back, I wonder why I wasted so much energy worrying about the quality of my vision. In retrospect, my vision, for all of its shortcomings must have been adequate. It wasn't a world-class, take-your-breath-away vision; I'll quickly admit that. Maybe most visions aren't world-class breath-takers. Maybe most Christians have garage-sale, black-and-white visions like mine.

Whatever the quality of my vision, it got me started. And that vision kept me going. So in the end it was good enough.

The interesting thing about that vision was that the reception got clearer over time. One year later I saw more than I did initially. Ten years later I could see the vision with added definition. Here's what I see now: I would never have seen the first worship service or anything that happened in the years that followed if I had not started moving forward with my fuzzy-reception vision.

The Power of More People with Vision

Could it be that God made us, all of us, naturally visionary? If so, we must think differently about vision. We must begin to think of vision as a natural part of living the Christian life. Consider the potential. Millions of Christians could build on that innate ability to be visionary. More Christians than we've ever dreamed possible could act on their visions and then function as leaders.

Why not pass the word around? It's OK to see what others don't see. Go ahead. Don't worry. You have a vision. Now get busy and make that vision a reality!

Here's a warning: Be careful. If you start seeing what doesn't exist and talking about what could be, others may see what you see. Keep talking, and others may get excited about what you see. They may begin to care about those things as you do. Before long those people may want to work with you to make that vision a reality. When that happens, you've set the process in motion. You've fired up the engine on the Leadership Train. Better get ready.

People will believe you're a leader. So get ready to lead.

. . . .

Planning: "How Do I Get to What I See?"

. . . .

LET'S SAY YOU HAVE AN IDEA. YOU SEE A NEED IN YOUR church. It bothers you that the need exists. That need causes thoughts and ideas to explode in your mind like microwave popcorn. You see possible ways to meet that need. You keep thinking about the need and find yourself saying, "Someone ought to do something about that situation."

If you've ever had feelings like these, you've had a vision. Probably you did not (and would not) feel comfortable calling your ideas a vision. To you they were just thoughts, ideas, or even dreams. You noticed some needs and started thinking about ways to meet them.

God made all of us visionary. We call the natural process you experienced *visioning.*

Like any ability God gives us, we must develop our visioning skills. God made you a natural visionary. God expects you, however, to become an effective visionary. Natural visionaries see things that need to change. Effective visionaries make things change.

Think of visioning as the engine of a train. Your natural ability to notice needs and picture possible ways to meet them produces a vision. Your vision becomes the engine. But it is an idle engine.

People may enjoy looking at a stationary train engine. Yet an idle engine pulls nothing. Someone needs to fire up the engine, connect it to a string of cars, and get it moving. You can learn to fire up your vision. You can learn the skills leaders use to harness the power of vision to produce change. Your vision can become a powerful engine in a Leadership Train.

Let's assume you have a vision, your engine. You have seen an unmet need and can picture possible ways to meet it. To fire up that engine, you need personal planning.

The Key Role of Personal Planning

You must do some personal planning before you ask people to ride your Leadership Train with you. The personal planning process accomplishes two key steps for you. First, personal planning will show if you have a vision worth your commitment, energy, and time. Second, personal planning will help you set the general direction you need to go.

Personal planning differs from group planning. After you commit to your vision and set a general direction, you'll enlist others. Together you and they will become a team. You will build teams by group planning. Group planning ensures that your vision becomes the team's vision. The group planning process will help clarify your initial vision. You need the group. The group, however, needs you to do some work first.

Vision needs personal planning for power. We've assumed you have a vision. Now let's analyze the two parts of the personal planning process: (1) your personal commitment, and (2) the general direction.

Personal Commitment in Planning

Your commitment to your vision and the general direction you set to reach it depend on how you answer the strategic question in the personal planning process: How do I get to what I see?

A powerful vision demands someone with a powerful commitment. You may have great ideas, valid ideas, even important ideas. You may correctly identify needs and think of valid ways to meet those needs. At that stage you have a vision—the engine. Unfortunately that engine will stand still until someone makes a powerful commitment to it. "Right," you say, "but does the someone have to be me?"

In a word, yes.

Beware! Danger lurks at this point. Before investing time in personal planning, some people try to hedge their bets, limiting their commitment to their vision.

These people think of themselves as "idea people." They enjoy identifying unmet needs and imagining ways those needs could be met. Some "idea people" consider their job complete once they articulate "visions." "I just create engines," they may say. "I don't get them moving."

Perhaps they take that idle engine—a vision without personal planning—to their church. They meet with their pastor or other church leaders. "Someone sure needs to drive this engine," they say. "Not me, of course, but someone. You probably ought to find someone; you probably ought to find someone soon!"

Well-intentioned Christians clutter churches with vision engines they create but don't want to drive. If you're ever tempted to delegate your vision, stop! Remember, God made you and everyone else visionary. That means they, like you, see unmet needs and think of ways to meet them. Chances are good they frustrate themselves with the visions they don't have time or energy to implement. Do them a favor. Drive your own vision engine!

So that brings us back to a key question: Are you committed to your vision? Personal planning will help answer that question.

Planning Focuses Visions

Personal planning takes time. If you're not willing to invest some time to define and develop your vision, that's fine. Don't, however, expect others to do what you're not willing to do. On the other hand, by spending some time—even limited time—in personal planning, you'll discover your level of commitment. You'll find that personal planning either makes you more excited, or you'll find yourself less interested in what you've seen.

You'll generate far more visions in your life than you can ever act on. Personal planning helps you focus on the visions, big or small, to which God wants you to commit your time and energy.

Personal planning involves gathering information. Learn all you can about your vision. Your goal is to piece together a map of the distance between where you are and where you want to be. You already know the unmet need at the heart of your vision; that's what pricked your initial interest. Plus, you have some general ideas about how to meet that need; those ideas prompted you to act. Personal planning, sketching out the map, builds on that foundation.

Start learning about your vision from every source you can find. Since God made everyone naturally visionary, chances are good that others have noticed a similar need and tried to meet it. Learn all you can from them. Listen to them. Ask questions. If they write, read it. If they give speeches, order recordings of their ideas. Attend seminars.

Try to meet with key people. Ask questions. Build on every bit of information you gather. Piece together your initial map. You must discover if it's possible to get to what you see. Better yet, you may decide there is more than one way to get there. There usually are several ways.

A Story of Personal Vision and Planning

In February 1987, David Palmer, then director for Church Extension for the Northwest Baptist Convention, called me from Portland, Oregon. At that time I was an associate pastor at First Baptist Church of Garland, Texas. David asked me to consider moving to Lake Oswego, Oregon (a suburb of Portland) to begin a mission church.

For almost nine years I had enjoyed my ministry in Garland. Yet my wife, Lynn Marie, and I had talked of someday leaving the Bible Belt and ministering in a different part of the country. We knew the great need for new churches. We sensed we might have the skills needed. We even had some vague ideas about what we would do to begin a new church. In a sense, we had a vision. It was, however, an idle vision, a vision going nowhere. David Palmer's call changed all that. Suddenly I had to decide if I could commit to such a vision and make the commitment required to implement it.

Personal planning became my action step. Initially I took the big step and commited to becoming a church planter. I didn't know enough about the process. I was, however, committed enough to learn more.

Over a two-month period I gathered every resource I could find about starting a new church. I read books. I read publications produced by various organizations. I listened to recordings by people who had started churches in California and Illinois. I talked to everyone I could find who had started churches. I interviewed people who had lived in the Northwest and started churches there. The more I learned, the more intrigued I became. My commitment to the idea of beginning a new church grew and grew.

At that point, however, I still kept my options open. The vision lured me; the vision terrified me. David Palmer from the Northwest Baptist Convention sensed this struggle and offered a suggestion. "Why don't you and Lynn Marie visit the Northwest for a few days?" he said. "We'll show you around, let you see the area. You'll not be making a commitment to come. You'll simply be coming to look."

Thinking back on his invitation after all these years, I recognize the importance of that trip my wife and I made to Portland. It was a step, but it was more. It was an essential step. For us that initial trip demonstrated that our growing vision had moved beyond the "nice idea" stage. Our commitment was growing. We sensed this vision could become our vision.

As we learned more about beginning a church in the Northwest, we found ourselves confused and often overwhelmed. All the same, the opportunity fascinated us. Ideas flooded as we discussed what we would do *if* we did start this new church. New ideas generated new questions to ask. Answered questions generated new ideas.

After four months of prayer, study, and gathering information, I knew two things. First, I had a mental picture of the type of church I felt could be effective in Lake Oswego, Oregon. Second, I had several general ideas about how we could begin such a church.

In June 1987, my wife and I settled the commitment issue. We felt this church planting vision was God's vision for us. We announced to our church in Garland that we would be leaving. We committed ourselves.

Westside Baptist Church held its first worship service ten months after our point of commitment. Those ten months were essential to all that our little church would ever be and do. I invested those months in more personal planning!

I wrote extensively, forcing myself to outline the vision I had for the new church and the values that would guide it. God even led me to an innovative church planting strategist in Los Angeles named Norm Whan who was refining a plan for starting churches through telemarketing. His ideas (actually his vision) proved to be *the* key part of the strategy we used to begin Westside. And I only learned about Norm through a piece of junk mail I received.

Leaders in the Northwest Baptist Convention compiled demographic data and marketing surveys on the area we would seek to reach. At times the collection of information threatened to overwhelm me.

Personal planning helped lay the foundation for our future church. Before we had our first service, before I enlisted people to join me, I struggled to answer the strategic question: How do I get to what I see? That struggle prepared me to enlist others to share my vision.

The personal planning process ensured my commitment to the vision. The more I learned, the more committed I became. The personal planning process helped me sketch the map we would use to travel toward the vision. The personal planning process helped me identify many routes, determine the ones to avoid, and focus on the ones that were possible alternatives.

Don't Be Intimidated by Planning

My story about personal planning describes one extreme. Fortunately, most visions do not require this level of planning. On a ten-point scale, what I just described is a ten, and most visions require far less personal planning. But even a one-point level of planning is important. A one-point level of planning moves you out of the ranks of the big talkers and into the circle of those who make a commitment and make things happen.

So don't let personal planning intimidate you. If you have a vision, test it. Gather resources. See what you can learn. Once you get started, one of two things will happen. You may find your interest fading. That may be God's way of leading you away from that vision and toward another one. On the other hand, you may find your commitment growing as you learn more. That's a sure sign you are moving in a promising direction. You may discover that you, in time, can answer the question, How do I get to what I see? Combine commitment and a general plan, and you have something powerful—a pulsing engine that can pull a Leadership Train! Now all you need is some other people to ride the train with you!

. . . .

Enlisting: "Would You Like to Go There with Me?"

. . . .

YOU HAVE A VISION; YOU SEE SOMETHING THAT NEEDS TO exist. You've completed your planning, thereby identifying the general route to your destination. These two elements, vision and planning, form the engine on your Leadership Train.

As a leader, you now reach a critical point. You must decide if you can reach your vision alone or if you will need other people to help. Most visions require more than you can do alone. Fulfilling your vision will depend on how well you enlist others to help. Vision and planning are the engine on your Leadership Train. Enlisting is the passenger car. You must answer a foundational question. How will you convince people to fill your passenger car and travel to your destination with you?

Four Types of People

There are four types of people you can seek to enlist:
- People who care about you but not your vision
- People who care about your vision but not you
- People who care about you and your vision
- People who don't really care about you or your vision

The type of people you seek to enlist influences your enlistment strategy. The type of people determines the level of involvement you can expect once you enlist them.

An Enlistment Miracle

During the fall of 1987, I faced the greatest enlistment challenge of my life. I envisioned a new church in Lake Oswego, Oregon, and sensed God had called me to start it. Having completed my personal planning, I decided to use an innovative church-starting telemarketing plan (Now is that weird or what?) named "The Phone's for You." The plan was developed by Norm Whan. I set an initial goal of making eighty thousand phone calls into our target area to discover prospects. I developed a plan to accomplish this dial-up goal: enlist people from my home church, First Baptist Garland, Texas, and train them to be "telemarketers for Jesus." My plan included asking them to make 100 to 150 long-distance calls from Texas to Oregon and pay their own phone bill. (Was that crazy or what?)

Working with Roger McDonald, then the senior pastor of First Baptist Garland, and David Francis, then the minister to adults, we enlisted our team of telemarketers. In January 1988 more than five hundred families spent 2,443 hours making 43,480 phone calls. They discovered 2,668 families in Portland interested in hearing about a new church in their area. Callers did indeed pay their own long-distance bills. (I still have stacks of phone bill receipts as souvenirs of their heroic and selfless efforts.) In March 1988, we all saw the results of their work as 209 people attended the first service of our new church.

Four Types of "Telemarketers for Jesus"

The more than five hundred families and individuals who made calls did so for different reasons. As you can guess, no one wanted to be a telemarketer. Yet they became home-based telemarketers. To understand why they made their calls, we can subdivide them into the four categories.

Callers Who Cared About Me but Not Necessarily About My Vision

I grew up at First Baptist Church, Garland, Texas, and actively participated in the life of the church until I left for college. I returned to the church as minister to youth while attending Southwestern Seminary. After seminary I became associate pastor at the church. I served on the pastoral staff of the church for over nine years. Combining growing up and staff years, I stacked up more than twenty-five years of relationships with the people of that wonderful church. So when I shared my Oregon Telemarketers for Jesus Vision, many immediately (and miraculously) said they would make calls simply because they cared about me.

Enlisting these people required little skill on my part and almost no persuasion. In a sense they weren't especially concerned with my vision. They didn't ask many questions about my strategy or my plans. In most cases they were not passionate about starting new churches. They simply loved me. So when I asked them to help me, they simply said, "Sure, I'll help."

If you need help in reaching your vision, look first to the people who love you. Be careful though; even these people will resist if they sense you are using them. However, if you have an established relationship of trust with them and you've not asked for help too many times in the past, you can expect their support.

Be realistic about what you ask them to do for you. Remember, they don't necessarily care about your vision. You and they will have a positive experience if you ask them to do something specific that allows them to express their love for you. Don't ask them for long-term involvement, though, on the strength of relationship alone. No matter how much they love you, in time they will begin to feel drained, even used. You need as many of these people in your passenger car as you can get. Just be realistic about why they are riding with you. Be prepared for them to board early but then get off at a station not far down the line.

Callers Who Cared About My Vision but Not Necessarily About Me

First Baptist Garland has, over the years, collected and developed a core of people passionate about missions. Through the missions organizations and missions involvement, they have nurtured a vision of reaching the world for Christ.

Among the five hundred were some people who didn't really know me. They listened as I described a need for a new church in Lake Oswego. Using long-distance telemarketing to plant a church captured their imagination. They sensed my commitment to planting the church and that I believed God had called me to do it. After listening and watching our plans unfold, many in this group said, "Yes, I'll help." They boarded my passenger car.

Those in this group don't have a strong relationship with you, so they will focus on your vision and plan. If you don't have a clear vision and a definite plan, they will usually decline to help. Since they share visions similar to yours, they are looking for ways to invest their time, energy, and money to fulfill those visions. They are evaluating your vision in the context of other opportunities to accomplish something similar. You are giving them options from which to choose, so you need to provide a strong option.

As you seek to enlist these people, ask yourself, "Why should these people help me?" The good news is that these people will listen to you. But it's up to you to articulate the vision, describe a definite plan, and present specific ways these people can help accomplish important goals. There is more good news: these kinds of people will want to help you. You're going where they want to go!

Be prepared as you work with these people. They bring passion, energy, and resources. Along the way, because they feel strongly about the vision, they will have definite ideas about what could and should be done. These people will board your Leadership Train in the passenger car. Down the track they'll stroll up to the engine and offer to help you drive. More than likely you'll need and want their help. They are the kind of people who will make the complete trip to your vision with you, as long as they sense you need them and the train moves in the right direction. Your relationship with them will grow over time, but don't confuse their initial motivation. They are there for the vision, not for you.

Callers Who Cared About Me and My Vision

Among the five hundred at First Baptist Garland was a group that every leader dreams of in enlistment. These people loved me *and* my vision. They combined the key elements of the previous two groups: they boarded the train early and stayed with me for the entire trip.

These people comprised an essential core of the team we sought to enlist and build. In our Telemarketers for Jesus project, these were the people who signed up to make calls as soon as we announced the project. Once the project began, these were the people who made two hundred, three hundred, and even more calls! In addition, many of these people traveled to Lake Oswego, Oregon, to be with us for the first service as our baby church was born. These were the people who continued to follow our progress, our ups and downs, for years to come, encouraging us and praying for us.

In your vision you'll need to enlist some people like this—people who love you and your vision. They are God's special gift to you. They'll join your team easily and stay with you for the duration. They'll do whatever you ask along the way, working with you to see the vision become reality. If you've spent time with people over the years, loved them, shared their dreams and vision, you should identify some people in this group. You'll need them. They will help you more than you can possibly imagine.

Callers Who Didn't Really Care About Me or My Vision

Our phone call strategy for beginning Westside through long-distance phone calls taxed First Baptist Garland, Texas, to the limits. Initially we wanted eight hundred families or individuals to make calls. Even for a large church, that was an unrealistic goal. Even with the five hundred, we involved many people who were less involved in the life of the church. For them, being Telemarketers for Jesus was their first involvement in ministry at the church.

Many of them boarded my Leadership Train and piled into my passenger car. However, they waited until the last minute to board, and some were tentative about their involvement throughout the project.

These people proved to be our greatest enlistment challenge. They didn't have a relationship with me. They didn't, in most cases, have any strong desire to start a church in Oregon through telemarketing. Yet they did work. They made the calls. We could not have implemented our strategy without them.

The key to enlisting these people was threefold: (1) enlist through others; (2) remove fears; and (3) provide support. Against all odds, these people came through and made an invaluable contribution to the project. One thing we learned was that this group tended to do a bit less than what we had hoped. Rather than make one hundred calls, many made fewer. Rather than calling for two or three nights, they called one night and turned in their results. Initially, I was disappointed, but in retrospect, I'm not. Instead, I'm amazed they made any calls at all. And in the end we would not have been successful without them.

A Textbook Case Study of Enlisting

David Francis, who was minister to adults at First Baptist Garland at that time, designed our strategy to enlist people. He used the adult Sunday school organization as the basis for enlistment. He asked department directors to enlist a team of callers from their departments. David designed and displayed status boards in the atrium of the church. Each board showed the number of callers each department had added to its team. Directors allowed David and me to speak in each adult department. We challenged them to get involved, answered questions, and removed fears.

This process continued for four months. Even after all that effort, the majority of the people didn't commit to make the calls until the day we offered training. Nonetheless, they came, committed, and called.

You'll need to work with people who don't really care about you or your vision. Enlisting them takes time and energy. Working with them after they sign up may provide more challenges. You'll need to enlist them through others. Work to remove fears they may have about being involved. Assure them they will receive the support needed for success.

They will help you fulfill your vision. They'll climb into your passenger car and ride your Leadership Train. You may struggle to get them on board and to keep them from getting off. Yet they will become key members of your team and make an invaluable contribution to your vision.

Who's in Your Passenger Car?

Vision identifies your destination. Planning lays out your initial strategy for making the trip. Enlisting identifies the four groups of people of whom you can ask this strategic question: "Would you like to go there with me?"

Some in each of the groups will say yes at different times, for different reasons, and with different levels of commitment. Persist with wisdom, and you'll fill your passenger car. With that task behind you, you're ready to start transforming that car of passengers into a team. That's the next challenge on your Leadership Train.

STEP FOUR

· ·

Team Building: "How Will We Get There?"

· ·

YOUR LEADERSHIP TRAIN IS MOVING. THE ENGINE—*VISION* and *personal planning*—pulls the other cars toward your ulti-mate destination. Vision and personal planning enable you to enlist people to make the journey with you. Through enlistment you fill the passenger car and lengthen your Leadership Train.

You're ready now for a new challenge: transforming the group of people in your passenger car into an effective team. Leaders call the skills you will need *team building.*

Five essential steps are part of the team-building process:

1. Deepen relationships
2. Clarify the vision
3. Identify individual strengths

41

4. Decide on the team strategy
5. Get started

1. Deepen Relationships

Teams develop as relationships deepen. Deepening relationships demand time. No shortcuts exist.

Many leaders, focused as they are on their visions, move directly from enlistment to working on the project. They consider taking time to deepen relationships a waste of time. In reality, more work will be done effectively if leaders take time in the beginning to deepen and solidify relationships among those they enlist.

People work together more effectively when they know one another and value their relationships. Unfortunately, busy schedules and cultural norms discourage anything but superficial relationships. With few opportunities for people to open their lives and tell their stories, relationships remain superficial.

Experienced leaders work to solve this problem. They create opportunities for group interaction. They give people permission to talk about themselves in a supportive environment.

Group members must move beyond simply stating personal facts: family status, occupation, or hobbies. Fact sharing starts the process. Deep relationships, however, require more than emotionally safe fact exchanges.

People need to share their faith story, how they came to Christ and how they feel about their spiritual life. People can tell their family story, something about their spouse, children, relatives, parents, plus the values and activities they associate with family. Telling their vocational story is also important, especially if it includes information about accomplishments that brought great satisfaction. Finally, people can share a painful story, telling about a disappointment or hurt that marked their lives positively or negatively. Although not a common practice in most groups, such sharing quickly adds depth to growing relationships.

Effective leaders set the pace in deepening relationships by sharing their stories. Group members carefully monitor what the leader shares. They watch the leader's openness. Leaders who share on a superficial, facts-only level build groups that share at that limited level. On the other hand, leaders who share with appropriate openness build teams who share with equal openness.

Time becomes a catalyst for deepening relationships. Leaders who want their teams to develop more quickly intensify and lengthen the amount of time their group spends together at the beginning of the project. If the group decides to meet only for a certain number of meetings, the leader may devote the entire first meeting to group sharing. For a major project, the leader may bring the people together for an extended time, such as a retreat. Even spending a long evening together eating, laughing, and sharing openly enables important relationships to develop in a relatively short time.

Leaders communicate their values through the emphasis they place on deepening relationships. Excellent leaders communicate this message: "We have important tasks to accomplish. But we also have the opportunity to build friendships. In time, we will complete our tasks. Our friendships can go on for years to come."

When people sense their leaders care for them as persons, not just workers, their commitment to the leader and the task grows. Wise leaders understand this reality and strive to make deepening relationships a top priority.

2. Clarify the Vision

You, as the leader, clearly focused on your vision at the beginning of your leadership process. Yet your group members can help you see the vision with increased clarity.

To become a team, group members need a sense of ownership in the project. Ownership grows as people struggle in group planning as you, the leader, struggled in personal planning.

Your developing team will appreciate the time you invested in personal planning before you enlisted them. They know the frustration of being enlisted to complete an ill-defined task with no clear plan. Your group members will bring their own ideas, opinions, and experiences. They will expect to work with you to shape a vision that together you will work to accomplish.

Be positive. Expect the group's ideas to clarify, not cloud, your vision. When people sense that you value their ideas, they will take another significant step toward thinking of themselves as a team.

3. Identify Individual Strengths

Discerning leaders recognize that each person brings important strengths to the team. Unfortunately, some of the enlisted members will not have clear or accurate ideas about their strengths. You, as the leader, can help them discover the strengths they bring to the group. More important, you can show them how those strengths are vital to the team's ultimate success.

Through the process of deepening relationships, you will gain insights into each individual's strengths. Take the next step by leading the group to identify the skills needed to implement the vision.

Focus the group on the destination you, as a group, want to reach. Start at the destination and work backward. Ask the group, "What skills will we need to make this a reality?" Begin to list all the individual tasks and skills crucial to success. Once completed, spend time discussing the skills and tasks on the list. Ask a question like, "Have any of you worked in situations that called for one of these skills?" Give group members a chance to talk. Listen. Remind group members that skills show up in unlikely and unrelated situations. As individual members share, write their names beside the skills identified.

After the discussion, group members should have a twofold awareness. First, they will know more about one another by understanding the experiences and skills members bring to the team. Second, they will have a greater appreciation for the team that is developing.

4. Decide on the Team Strategy

By this time in the team-building process, your group should appreciate the other members of the group, understand the vision the group seeks to accomplish, plus recognize some strengths each person brings to the team. Now the team must focus on the specific strategy it will use.

Effective leaders guide their teams like a good football coach. The leader helps the group draw all the information into focus: the vision, the individual strengths of the team members, and the collective skills they as a team possess. Leaders then work with the team to finalize the strategy.

This strategy began when the leader crafted plans as part of personal planning. Now specific plans must be made that maximize the strengths their team possesses.

These plans resemble a coach's playbook. Each play is tailor-made for the strengths of his team. Only an inexperienced coach designs plays calling for quickness and speed when his team's strengths are power and size.

You, as the leader, can ask for additional "plays" from your team. More than likely your team members will have ideas about how to reach the vision. Recognize, however, that ultimately you are responsible for the final plan. You will take all you have learned in the team-building process and finalize the strategy. In the end you will have to say, "Here's what we're going to do."

If your team is developing well, they will receive your suggestions with excitement. Of course, they will evaluate the strategy you suggest. They may continue to offer suggestions to fine-tune what you present. In the end we hope they will say, "I can see our team doing that."

If by some chance you present your strategy and your team has more questions than enthusiasm, you'll need to slow down. Spend more time talking, listening, and sharing. Don't be too concerned. Even such a reevaluation process enhances team building. In time your group will understand the "plays" and feel confident in their design. When that time comes, you're ready to move into the crucial part of the team-building process.

5. Get Started!

Teams play the game. No alternative exists. A group of athletes has a vision of winning the game. But if they never played a game, they wouldn't be a team. A group could have an elaborate book of offensive and defensive plays. But if they never ran the plays during a real game, they would not be a team. It will be the same way in your team-building challenge. Ultimately you will say to your team, "Let's get into the game."

Leaders expect challenges as their team begins working. Well-crafted plays sometimes prove disastrous in the real game. Problems are inevitable. Only when we start can we identify problems and make adjustments. In the end, playing the game becomes the most important part of team building. Ultimately, people become a team by working as a team.

New Church Team Building

As the pastor of a new church in Lake Oswego, Oregon, I learned about this team-building process as we started working to begin our adult Sunday school organization. During the early days of our church, we attracted new Christians or reactivated Christians with no leadership experience. No one felt comfortable leading Bible studies. Few felt comfortable in roles as Christian leaders. Yet key individuals began to emerge as natural leaders. People expected them to lead, and they did so in a positive fashion.

In time I enlisted these people as our small-group leaders. Together we discussed my vision for the ministry of

Bible study and fellowship. I shared my ideas. They shared their ideas and fears! We deepened our relationships. We identified necessary tasks and skills. We talked about possible strategies. Finally we got started.

Initially our groups were fellowship groups. Since we had no Bible teachers, we began with the strengths we had—a group with strong people skills. Helping people develop relationships in our church became our first priority. We recognized our need to bond people through friendships. Without friends, they wouldn't stay with us long enough to experience the Bible study program we hoped to develop.

For four months we struggled along with four groups of adults meeting primarily for fellowship. These groups were far from perfect, but they got us started. During this time we refined our vision and our strategy. We identified and trained Bible study leaders.

After four months of sputtering along, we launched a full Sunday school organization with four adult departments. A perfect Sunday school it wasn't. But it was a start.

Over time that Sunday morning Bible study program became a vital part of our church. We made progress. We continually faced new struggles. Fortunately our leadership group had become a team. They became a team, in part, because of the struggles we faced together!

Back to the Leadership Train

Are you ready to get your Leadership Train moving? You'll need the powerful engine that develops through vision and personal planning. These two make effective enlistment possible. You'll need to transform the group in your passenger car into an effective team. The five-step team-building process will require fuel. So prepare to hook up the fuel car next. A full fuel-load of communication and delegation will enable you, as the leader, to keep your Leadership Train moving toward your ultimate vision.

. . . .

Communication: "What Do You See?"

. . . .

TRAINS WILL NOT RUN WITHOUT FUEL. LEADERS CANNOT lead and teams will not work without communication. Compare the leadership process to a train, and communication becomes fuel in the train's fuel car.

Leaders communicate. They communicate the destination toward which they are moving. *Visioning* and *personal planning* create a picture of the destination and a general plan to get there. However, only communication moves that picture from the mind of the leader to the minds of those who board the passenger car through *enlistment*.

Team building requires communication. Leaders communicate with their team. Leaders guide team members to communicate with one another. Communication makes the team's group planning process possible and productive.

Every facet of leadership requires communication. Yet effective communication remains as elusive as a four-year-old in a Christmas toy store. Talking—that's easy. Communicating—that's the challenge.

Communication becomes complicated because people are different. They respond to other people differently. They gather information differently. They make decisions differently. They approach life differently.

Ineffective leaders assume that all people are the same. They generally think that everyone is just like they are. These leaders communicate to others in only one way, their way. Effective leaders recognize that people are different. They work to understand these differences and communicate in ways each person prefers.

A helpful tool in understanding some of the differences in people is the book *Please Understand Me: Character and Temperament Types* by David Keirsey and Marilyn Bates. The book explains the popular Myers-Briggs Type Indicator, a psychological assessment tool used sometimes in business settings. In simple terms Keirsey and Bates explain four general ways in which people differ. They even provide a simple instrument that helps people discover and understand their differences.

Over the years, in church and in business, I used this tool to help adjust my leadership and communication to match the unique needs of individuals and groups. We even used this tool in our mission church. Our people enjoyed learning about themselves and one another. What we learned together helped all of us—and especially me, as the leader—communicate more effectively!

Keirsey and Bates focus on four general differences in people. The first three directly influence the way we communicate:

1. Extroversion . . . Introversion
2. Sensing . . . Intuition
3. Thinking . . . Feeling
4. Structured . . . Unstructured

(Note: Rather than "structured" and "unstructured," Keirsey and Bates use the terms "judging" and "perception." Some teams I've worked with found those terms confusing, so I use the alternate terms.)

Let's look at the first three areas of difference in people and consider how each impacts communication.

Extroversion . . . Introversion

This describes the way people gather emotional energy. People who find themselves invigorated and renewed through contact with people are classified as *extroverts*. People who find themselves invigorated and renewed through solitude are classified as *introverts*. A study conducted in 1964 found that 75 percent of us are extroverts and 25 percent of us are introverts.

The classifications *extrovert* and *introvert* do not refer to social skills, enjoyment of people, or effectiveness in working with people. Instead these classifications describe what happens to people when they are with people.

The longer extroverts are with people, the more energy they have. Solitude drains them! The longer introverts are alone, the more energy they have. People drain them!

Once my wife and I hosted a potluck dinner at our home for ten couples who were key leaders in our church. As part of our evening together, I asked each person to complete the simple assessment included in the book *Please Understand Me: Character and Temperament Types.* I told them I would score their assessments and then discuss the results at our next leadership meeting.

Our evening together began at 6:30 with dinner and included good food, lively conversation, laughter, and playing a popular board game. At about 9:15, an appropriate break in the activities occurred, and about half the couples left.

The half that remained encouraged me to score the assessments and tell them the results. I did and then explained the various classifications. After a few minutes of talking about our scores, a humorous truth became clear. Everyone who remained after the 9:15 exodus scored on the assessment as extroverted. We quickly looked at the other assessments and confirmed our hunch. Our friends who left at 9:15 scored as introverts.

There was one exception to this that got a laugh from the collection of extroverts. I scored as an introvert on the assessment. The joke was that I would have left at 9:15 if the party had not been at my house! The extroverted group encouraged me to go to my room if I began to feel drained! They, under the leadership of my extroverted wife, had a grand time talking, laughing, and sharing until close to midnight. As soon as the group left, I stumbled toward bed in a near-coma from introvert-interaction overload.

Communication becomes more effective when leaders understand their team members and can identify the extroverts and introverts. Extroverts thrive on brainstorming sessions and extended times together. The longer extroverts talk, the better they feel. On the other hand, introverts find that same experience draining. They need people in small doses.

Effective leaders vary the settings they use for communication. On occasion they gather the team together and allow the group to interact and talk their way to understanding. Other times leaders communicate in a directed manner, presenting a block of information to the group. They then close the meeting and allow people time alone to think through the information.

Variety often leads to effectiveness. There are no right and wrong ways. There are only helpful and less helpful ways. What is helpful depends on whether you are an extrovert or an introvert.

Sensing . . . Intuition

People think about life's issues in different ways. Those classified as *sensing* focus on information through the five senses. These people want facts, and they trust experience. On the other hand, those classified as *intuitive* enjoy thinking by using images and metaphors and by focusing on the future. They get hunches and may speak of having a "sixth sense." A 1964 study indicated that 75 percent of us are "sensing" and 25 percent of us are "intuitive."

A congregational meeting in our church illustrated the roles sensing and intuition play in communication. Bob, the head of our finance committee, presented information about our church finances. He included a complete, three-page computer spreadsheet of our projected budget. It accurately depicted our past financial experience and even projected the implication of that experience over the next two years. The material was clear, concise, and accurate.

I watched people as Bob made his presentation. Many in the congregation had a wonderful time interacting non-verbally with Bob as he spoke. During the question time, they asked appropriate, penetrating questions that indicated their understanding of what he presented.

Other people's faces and questions told a different story. They stared with puzzled expressions as Bob spoke. They fumbled with pages, continually looking over at their neighbor's sheet to discover which page Bob was discussing. The few who asked questions revealed great confusion and frustration. Even after Bob tried to answer their questions, questions remained.

After the meeting, one of our most encouraging intuitive members came up to me. After every sermon I preached or meeting I led, she tried to say something positive. That day she smiled at me and said, "John, that was so well done. I appreciate Bob's hard work. I'm sure those who enjoy that sort of thing truly enjoyed it." And with that, she grinned. I understood her joke.

She recognized that our sensing people had enjoyed the morning. She and other intuitive people had not! However, because our people were beginning to understand their differences, no one complained. They knew we would find other ways to communicate with our intuitive friends. The sensing folks had their day. Our intuitives knew their day would come.

A key step in effective communication is to determine if you, as a leader, are a sensing person or an intuitive person. Whichever type you are, you'll have to work hard to communicate with people who have the other preference.

If you are a sensing person, you must learn to take facts and experience and find analogies and images that help your intuitive team members understand. If you are an intuitive person, you must take time to gather and focus on the facts that undergird experience. Otherwise, you will frustrate your sensing team members.

Continually monitor the way you communicate. If you use the same form of communication every time, you're frustrating people on your team. Shift your focus. Work to bring balance. Your team will appreciate your efforts.

Thinking . . . Feeling

People process information and make decisions in different ways. Those classified as *thinking* tend to make objective, impersonal, logical decisions. Those classified as *feeling* tend to make personal, values-based decisions. Assessment results indicate that these two preferences divide evenly across the general population, with slightly more women than men falling into the feeling category.

Effective communication increases when leaders understand these two types of people and draw on the strengths of each.

The leadership team of our church contained almost an equal number of thinkers and feelers. In those days I tended to present things from a thinking perspective. My approach rallied our thinkers and silenced our feelers. In the early months of our church, this imbalance created problems.

As our adult fellowship groups began to grow, I wanted to divide one of the largest groups to provide opportunities for greater growth. I had all the data to support my decision—experience, studies, facts. My feeling leaders, however, expressed concerns about the way people would feel if we implemented my ideas at that time. I discounted their ideas as overreacting. Of course, my thinking leaders totally agreed with me!

With the sensitivity of a buzz saw, I set the process in motion and divided the group. Problems immediately erupted. Group members expressed pain and anger. Feeling leaders expressed frustration with me for failing to heed their warning.

Fortunately, we adjusted, and I learned some vital lessons that helped me avoid problems in the future.

From that point on, when I met with our leadership team, I recognized my thinking bent. I counted on my feeling leaders to balance my focus on what was objective and logical. They, in turn, looked to me and our other thinkers to help them see the big picture and not lose perspective while trying to make everyone happy.

Even the struggles and missteps in the early days of our church made us stronger because we discovered how desperately we needed one another. When we took the time to talk about plans and sought to understand the objective and emotional sides of those plans, we made better decisions. We communicated.

To communicate effectively, you must discover if you are a thinker or a feeler. If you are a thinker, identify the feelers on your team. Tell them your ideas and plans. Then ask them to help you understand how your plans will make others feel. Ask them to help you respond to others in a sensitive way. Encourage them to tell you if they sense you have hurt others' feelings. If you are a feeler, identify the thinkers on your team. Ask them to help you see the big picture. Encourage them to tell you if you're becoming too focused on pleasing a few people at the expense of the larger group. Ask them to help you evaluate your plans. Work with them to word your plans in a way other thinkers will understand and appreciate.

We Need Each Other!

First Corinthians 12 affirms the fact that we all need one another. In that chapter Paul describes the church as a body with interdependent parts. The body cannot function without each part doing its job! Each part is different but necessary.

Paul focused on spiritual gifts as one basis for the differences between people. It may be that spiritual gifts are simply one aspect of the wonderful diversity God built into his body, the church. Through spiritual gifts, through temperament and personality type, God created us with complementary differences. As we value our differences, we will maximize our potential.

Back to the Leadership Train

In the leadership process, communication asks a strategic question, "What do you see?" Effective leaders recognize that God enables people to see the world differently. The best leaders work hard to understand and affirm those differences in each team member. Understanding people and learning to see the world through their eyes will help you see your ultimate destination more clearly. Clear vision will keep your Leadership Train moving down the track.

STEP SIX

....

Delegation: "What's Your Responsibility?"

....

MOVING YOUR LEADERSHIP TRAIN DOWN THE TRACKS toward your destination requires a variety of skills. Your skills in visioning and personal planning work like a powerful train engine; they get things moving. Your skills in enlisting and team building are like adding a passenger car to your train. They ensure you have the workforce needed to carry out your vision. You won't go far without fuel. Your skills in communication and delegation become the fuel car resources you will draw on throughout your journey.

As a leader, you must have workers, not just passengers. When you delegate, you ensure that every passenger on your train becomes a worker. In delegation you ask a strategic question: "What's your responsibility?" By asking the question, you affirm each member on your team. You are saying, "I'm glad you're here. We need you. Here's what I need you to do." Effective delegation assumes that your team members expect to work. They simply need direction.

Avery Willis provided a helpful framework for the delegation process in his book *MasterBuilder: Multiplying Leaders.* He presents six steps leaders can follow to ensure effective delegation:

1. Decide if the task can be delegated.
2. Use delegation to motivate.
3. Explain the task and ask the person's view.
4. Agree on the amount of responsibility and authority.
5. Agree on a set time for review.
6. Ask for a summary and pledge support.

Let's look at these six steps. We'll see how each builds on the next to ensure effective delegation.

Can This Be Delegated?

Delegation demands balance. You as the leader must balance the task and the people. In theory you can delegate any task to any person. Responsible leaders, however, recognize that people have strengths and limitations. In turn these leaders strive to delegate so people work on tasks they can do well. Everyone wins. The task is accomplished. People experience success.

Leaders can begin with a *task focus.* They ask, "Is this person the best one to work on this task?" Every team has members who are willing to work on a task yet do not have the skills to achieve desired results. The best leaders recognize that delegating the task to these people will hurt everyone—the project, the team, and ultimately the person. Knowing this, effective leaders take a stand, sometimes an unpopular stand. They say, "This task is important. We must entrust it to someone who can achieve these results."

Balance is necessary. The task focus combines with a *people focus.* Leaders ask, "Would working on this task be good for this person?" Your team may have several people with the necessary skills for a particular task. Your challenge then becomes matching the person and the task. If effective, you'll focus on a person saying, "I think Susan has the skills for this task and would enjoy doing it." When you can make that sort of statement, you know you have a task that can be delegated effectively.

One word of caution is in order. Some leaders keep too many tasks for themselves. They do so for a variety of reasons. Some worry that team members do not have needed skills. Their assessment may be accurate. Then again, it's possible to underestimate the skills of a particular person. In that case you may need to delegate and then watch closely to see how the person performs.

Other leaders worry that team members will not want to work on the delegated task. The leader may feel guilty about delegating, concerned that the team member feels the leader is dumping work rather than doing it.

Leaders must monitor their personal motives. Be candid with yourself and ask, "Am I delegating this task just because I don't want to do it?" If so, your team members will sense that motive and resent it.

Effective leaders avoid these problems. They work right along with their team members. They do the work, even the unpleasant tasks. With that background your team will respond positively when you ask them to accomplish a task for you.

A few leaders delegate too much. Far more leaders delegate too little. As a general rule, the answer to the question, Can I delegate this? is yes. Effective delegation, however, depends on what you do after you decide to delegate.

This Is Perfect for You!

Let's assume you have identified a task that can be delegated. You have a person on your team with the skills to accomplish the desired results. How you tell the person about the task you want accomplished will influence the effectiveness of your delegation.

When you delegate, you can encourage your team member. You can say to him, "Bill, I've been thinking about implementing our plan, and your name kept coming to mind as someone who could do a great job. I would like to tell you about one of the tasks and see if you would be willing to work on it."

Even if Bill decides he doesn't want to work on the task you suggest, you still win. Bill knows you have been thinking about him and value his abilities. More than likely Bill will respond even more favorably to you in the future.

Unfortunately this positive approach to delegation doesn't always happen in churches. For example, an ineffective leader may call Mary and say, "Mary, we haven't been able to get anyone to lead our junior high class next quarter. I've called seven others, and no one will help. Mary, I really need you to bail me out of this mess."

Will Mary be motivated by that approach to delegation? No, Mary will feel used. In fact, even if Mary says yes this time, it's likely she'll say no next time. She will remember and resent the way she received her task the last time.

Delegation provides a wonderful opportunity to affirm and motivate people. Take the time to meet with the person you have identified. Explain why you want her to work on this task. Tell her why you feel she could do an excellent job. She will probably feel motivated to work on the task. At the very least she will feel affirmed that you cared enough to think of her.

Here's What I See

If interested at all, your team member will ask for more information. At that point, you can respond in two ways:

1. Describe the process.
2. Describe the results.

If the task requires specific steps to achieve the desired results, you must describe them to your team member. On occasion this type of delegation is necessary, even effective. It's possible, though, for your team member to sense that all you want is a gopher—someone to "go fer" this and "go fer" that. If he senses that, he may be insulted. He may feel you don't trust him or value his ideas. Or he may agree to take the task but then come to you at each step along the way, seeking your approval. If this occurs, you must ask yourself if you have truly delegated the task at all.

Delegation becomes more effective and motivational to the worker if you focus on desired results, not the process. You as the leader entrust the task to the team member. You clarify the results you desire but expect the worker to develop the process.

For this type of delegation to be effective, you must explain clearly the results you expect. You must draw the target you expect your team member to hit. Too often leaders attempt delegation without drawing the target. Then when their team member produces results, the leader responds, "That's not really what I had in mind." Effective delegation requires a definite target. Give your team member that target, and entrust her to find the process to produce the desired results.

Once you describe the target, you should take time to let your team member express his feelings and ideas. Ask him, "Do you have any idea how you may work to achieve the results I've described?" Guard against slipping into "gopher delegation" at this point. Allow your team member to express ideas, even fears. You can meet again to discuss his specific plans. At this stage, you simply want to determine his response to what you have said. The person may simply say, "I don't know exactly how I will do it, but I'm sure willing to try." That's fine. You have moved well into the delegation process.

You're Authorized and Responsible!

Your team member needs to know how much authority she has in the delegated task. If, for example, you have a budget for your project, you can say, "Judy, we have $125 budgeted for this. As you need to make purchases, we will provide the funds up to that amount. If you spend more than that, we can't reimburse you." By stating this, you've given Judy the authority to spend money to accomplish her task, up to a point. You can also give her authority to enlist other workers, to establish plans, and to schedule events. You as the leader must decide the amount of authority you delegate with the task.

Remember that you must delegate the authority necessary for your team member to accomplish the task. Define the amount of authority you give, and ensure the team member understands how much or how little authority he has. Clearly state, "You can do this much on your own. If you go beyond this point, see me." These boundaries encourage team members. They know what they can and cannot do.

With authority comes responsibility. Effective leaders remind team members of this fact. In delegation it's appropriate to say: "I'm entrusting this to you. I'm counting on you. This part of our project is your responsibility." Most people work best when they feel responsible. Don't hesitate to help people feel responsible as you delegate the task to them.

Keep Me Posted on Your Progress

Most people on your team will feel some fears as they consider working on a task. They need the confidence that comes through knowing you will be involved with them. Instill this confidence as you delegate.

Affirm to your team members that you, as the leader, care about the accomplishment of this task. It may be helpful to agree on a formal schedule of when you will meet together to check progress. You could say, "Judy, why don't we plan to meet at least once a week while you're working on this? That will help me know how things are developing.

Plus, you'll have a time to tell me how I can help you." By establishing a specific time for progress reports, you encourage team members to bring several matters to you at one time. This protects you from the constant interruptions of a string of small problems. Of course, you want your team member to know that if problems develop that require attention, she can come to you any time. This open-door policy ensures that team members can work with confidence. They have a safety net under them. They know that if they need you, you'll be there and ready to help.

Have I Communicated?

You may find it helpful to end the delegation process by asking the person to summarize the things you have discussed. This may feel awkward to you. In reality, it can be natural if you handle it correctly. You can say, "Judy, we've talked about a number of things. Let me see if I've communicated well. Why don't you summarize what we've talked about today and what you're planning to do with this project."

If such an approach is not comfortable for you, feel free to take the lead yourself. You can say, "Judy, we've talked about a number of things. Let me summarize what we've talked about. Then you tell me if I've left out anything or misunderstood anything you've said." At that point simply state what you have discussed. Focus on the results you desire and the authority and responsibility you are entrusting. Usually, your team member will agree with what you have summarized. If she corrects or adds to what you say, your delegation process will be even more effective.

An Unending Process

If no one follows you, you are not a leader. If you want people to work, not just follow you, you must delegate. Delegation disperses the work that needs to be done to the people who can do it best. As a leader, you have an unending number of tasks to accomplish. You have a growing number of people on your team. Add those together, and you have an unending need to delegate.

Delegation transforms the passengers on your Leadership Train into workers. Delegate effectively, and those workers will help you reach your destination! Isn't that why you fired up the engine in your Leadership Train? Then delegate!

STEP SEVEN

....

Motivation:
"Why Did You Say Yes?"

....

PEOPLE ARE INTERNALLY MOTIVATED. MOTIVATION FLOWS from within people, like lava pouring from a volcano. Leaders may sometimes remove obstacles which hinder motivation in others. In the end, however, people are motivated for reasons only they understand—and sometimes for reasons even they do not grasp. You, as a leader, must understand the motivational forces that propel people into action.

As the engineer on your Leadership Train, you have fired up a powerful engine through visioning and personal planning. You hooked up your passenger car when you enlisted and worked on team building. You ensured adequate fuel for the long trip by filling the fuel car with your skills in communication and delegation. Now you're ready for the equipment car and the first of its key leadership skills—motivation.

The secret of motivation lies behind the words *yes* and *no.* When you ask team members to work, they will respond by saying either yes or no. Inexperienced leaders often take yes responses as a sign of motivation. Likewise, they assume that no responses show a lack of motivation. Unfortunately, the motivation process is complex. To understand motivation, you must ask: "Why did this person say yes?" or "Why did this person say no?" When you understand the reason for the response, you discover the motivational force. There are at least seven motivational forces to consider.

1. Ability
2. Satisfaction
3. Pleasure
4. Compulsion
5. Obligation
6. Values
7. Relationships

1. Ability: "I Can Do That"

When you ask team members to accomplish a task, some say yes because ability is their motivational force. They evaluate the task in light of their skills and say, "I can do that." They are not saying the work is satisfying or enjoyable. They are simply assessing their skill level against the skills the task requires. Ability as a motivational force is an essential part of sustained motivation. Without the confidence that comes with ability, few people will begin a task.

2. Satisfaction: "I Do That Well"

Other team members say yes to an assignment because satisfaction is their motivational force. They evaluate the task and agree to tackle it because they believe the work will bring satisfaction. Often these people have worked on similar tasks in the past, done them well, and felt good about their involvement. Past performance and a positive experience motivate them to say yes once again because they believe the new project will bring similar satisfying results.

3. Pleasure: "I Enjoy Doing That"

When you see team members initiating tasks, you may discover that pleasure is their motivational force. People gravitate toward tasks they enjoy. Recurring activity says, "I enjoy doing this." Usually pleasure, ability, and satisfaction combine as motivational forces in this case. People enjoy their task because they have the ability to do it well, enjoy it, and receive satisfaction in the process.

4. Compulsion: "I Must Do That"

Some team members say yes to an assignment because compulsion is their motivational force. Their yes response reflects motivation, but it is motivation with no alternative. The person believes he or she has no choice. Either an authority figure or circumstances dictate what must be done. For example, some people go to work each morning under compulsion with no other motivational force supporting their action. Compulsion can be effective in creating a force for action. Over time, however, compulsion alone grinds people down and discourages them.

5. Obligation: "I Should Do That"

Team members sometimes say yes because of obligation. This motivational force resembles compulsion but differs from it. Compulsion flows from an outside source. Obligation springs from within the individual. This person answers yes because to him or her the action is right. A person may believe others expect the action and failure to act would make him or her a "bad person." Obligation is a powerful motivational force within people. Like compulsion, obligation may become a negative force, especially if it is not paired with other positive forces such as satisfaction.

6. Values: "I Want to Do That"

When you describe essential tasks to your team, some say, "Yes, I'll do that." The motivational force behind their yes rests in their values. For reasons you cannot control and they may not even understand, the task you describe appeals to them. In their hierarchy of priorities, the task sounds important, valuable. Values are people's most significant motivational force. Over time people do what they value.

7. Relationship: "I Would Do That for You"

As you lead your team, you may be surprised when some individuals say yes to certain tasks. They tackle the work with enthusiasm even if skills and satisfaction are limited. In this case, you often find relationship is the motivational force. They say yes because they want to please you. Relationship can be a powerful motivational force. People do extraordinary things for people they love, revere, or respect. But problems can occur if people work on tasks on the basis of relationship motivation alone. Over time they often become frustrated if they lack skills and satisfaction.

Strategies for Impacting Motivational Forces

Although people are internally motivated, effective leaders work to influence the motivational process. Here are seven strategies that can help you impact the motivational forces in people's lives:

1. Increase skills through training.

When you provide specific skills training for your team members, you strengthen ability as a motivational force in their lives. Some team members say no when you ask them to complete a task because they doubt their skills. When you train your team members, you remove an obstacle that can block the flow of motivation. Training doesn't ensure motivated action. Training makes it more likely your team members will look at a task and say, "I can do that."

2. Probe past work for hints of satisfaction.

Guide people to tasks that satisfy them. To do so, you must identify such tasks. No shortcuts exist. You must take the time to know your team members, discuss their past work, and discover the frustrations and satisfaction of various tasks.

Many people have never evaluated their past work and ministry. Perhaps they can identify tasks they completed with satisfaction. They may not, however, be able to tell you why they felt satisfied. You'll need to ask a question like, "Why do you feel good about that project and not this other one?" Or ask, "In the last five years, what task do you remember with the greatest feeling of satisfaction? Why?"

Once you understand the tasks that bring satisfaction, you can guide your team toward similar tasks. Even this process cannot ensure motivated action. Your chance of unleashing motivation in your team improves, however, if you understand what has prompted satisfaction as the motivational force in the past.

3. Watch the actions people initiate.

If you know which tasks your team members enjoy, you have a good chance of directing their motivated action. Remember that people tend to do what they enjoy. Simply watch the tasks team members initiate. Watch for patterns of activity. Study your team members. Discuss what you observe. Ask a question like, "I've noticed your work in several areas recently and appreciate what you do. Could you tell me why you decided to get involved in these activities?"

Over time you'll understand how pleasure works as a motivational force in your team members' lives. If you can discover even a few tasks individuals enjoy, your chance of guiding their motivated action dramatically improves.

4. Ensure that people have choices when possible.

Protect people from working under compulsion by discussing the choices they have. Affirm that you appreciate their involvement in the ministry. Discuss other ministries that are available. If they want to serve in another ministry, help them explore that opportunity. If they want to serve in a different way within your current project, discuss other tasks they could tackle. Search for alternatives and choices. Free them from the ball and chain of compulsion that forces service because no alternative exists.

5. Release people from man-made obligations.

Christians can work with a healthy sense of obligation to God. We take many difficult steps because such actions are "right." For example, we work to love a difficult coworker even if we don't enjoy the process or find it satisfying. We act in love because of our relationship with Christ. In a positive sense, we feel obligated to base our life and actions on Christ's plan.

On the other hand, man-made obligations must be identified and confronted. Assure team members that they are not obligated to work in a particular ministry. If Christ has called and gifted them for that ministry, their obligation is to Him. Encourage them to please Christ, not you or anyone else in your church. Removing the obligation obstacle can help people find positive sources of motivation that will sustain them.

6. *Study behavior to discover values.*

Remember that people over time do what they value. Watch what your team members do first when they begin a series of tasks. Watch the tasks they tackle with tenacity. Listen to them talk about various tasks. Which do they consider most important? Which do they assert should be the team's highest priority? All these actions and comments provide clues about the person's values. As you identify the actions people value, you can ask them to do tasks in those areas. Encouraging people to work in areas they value assures powerful, sustained motivation.

7. *Lead on the basis of unconditional love.*

Affirm to your team that your love for them is unconditional. You appreciate all they do, but you love them no matter what they do. Assure them that they do not have to work to earn a close relationship with you.

Be prepared for such unconditional love to prompt an even stronger motivational force based on relationship. Such a force is positive. Jesus released motivation constantly in people through unconditional love. As a result, His disciples and others worked to please Him. As you build your relationship with your team members, they will respond with increasingly strong motivation.

Leadership Means Understanding People

Effective leaders understand people. They ask questions. They observe. When people say, "Yes, I'll do that task," effective leaders wonder why the person said yes. Effective leaders can discover the motivational forces in people's lives and cooperate with those forces to maximize internal motivation, an essential component of effective leadership.

Correction: "Is Something Wrong Here?"

How do you respond when a member of your team moves off in the wrong direction? What if he takes actions that may hurt him or others on your team?

Effective leaders monitor their team members' work. If problems develop, these leaders move quickly to find a solution and direct the person into positive activity. We call this response *correction*. Correction may be leadership's most challenging skill.

Author Avery Willis provided a helpful framework for the leadership skill of correction. Those who work with

people needing correction appreciate the practical guidelines provided.

Most people shy away from correcting anyone.
However, leaders must at times correct. Since that is true,
we must learn effective correction. Focusing on the following five areas will help:

1. Analyze the situation.
2. Choose a method.
3. Apply the method chosen.
4. Nurture the relationship.
5. Monitor the results.

1. Analyze the Situation

"Convince me that I have to do this." That's the kind of
statement many people make when faced with the need to
correct a member of their team. There are at least six questions you can ask as you prepare to deal with a problem. By
the time you answer all six questions, you can confront the
situation with perspective and conviction.

The first question is *what?* You can ask, "Is this the
right problem to correct?" Leaders create problems if they
confront the wrong issue or a symptom rather than the root
problem. Correction is always hard. Ensure that you are
working on the true problem.

The second question is *why?* You can ask, "Is this the
right reason?" Emotions can cloud your judgment. Are you

confronting because you are angry? Is the Holy Spirit leading you to talk with the person? You may identify a real
problem. But if you are dealing with it for the wrong
reasons, you may create problems rather than solve them.

The third question is *who?* You can ask, "Am I the right
person to do it?" Often you will identify a real problem that
needs attention and determine that you could deal with the
matter objectively. However, you may feel that you don't
know the person well enough to talk about the issue. You
may lack credibility. You may lack the biblical knowledge
to guide the person to what Scripture says about the matter. If so, you need to enlist someone else to do the work of
correction while you take a supportive role.

The fourth question is *when?* You can ask, "Is this the
right time to correct?" Leaders err in two extremes: moving
too quickly and waiting too long. If you move too quickly,
you may intercept a problem in the process of being
resolved. If so, you may hinder the resolution process. On
the other hand, if you wait too long, the problem may grow,
causing greater damage. Timing becomes a key issue.

The fifth question is *where?* You can ask, "Where is the
right place?" Correction always provides a relational challenge. If people become embarrassed or humiliated by the
presence of others, problems compound. Wise leaders wait
until correction can be done in a private setting, unhurried,
not strained. Optimum settings can be illusive. Experienced
leaders work to create the right setting and refuse to settle
for less.

The sixth question is *how?* You can ask, "How should I deal with this problem?" Correction must be appropriate. Experienced leaders carefully analyze the problem they are facing and confront the problem at an appropriate level.

After you analyze the situation, you're ready to choose the method of correction that is appropriate based on the problem you seek to address.

2. Choose a Method

Second Timothy 3:16–17 provides a guideline in choosing a method in correction. "All Scripture is inspired by God and is profitable for teaching, for rebuking, for correcting, for training in righteousness, so that the man of God may be complete, equipped for every good work."

A medical analogy can help unlock the meaning of the four key words in this passage. We can think of *teaching, training, correcting,* and *rebuking* as different approaches a doctor takes in dealing with a patient.

Teaching is like preventive medicine. Doctors suggest certain procedures designed to prevent future problems. In the same way, following God's directives as revealed in the Bible provides guidelines for living that protect us from future problems. When choosing a method, one key question is, Do I need to teach some biblical truth?

Training is like medicine prescribed for a specific problem. Often God's truth in the Bible must confront problems already developing in our lives. Detected early, these problems can be addressed, actions changed, and future problems avoided. When choosing a method, another key question is, Do I need to train in how to live?

Correction is like a curative surgical procedure. A doctor detects a relatively serious problem demanding attention. She moves quickly to deal with it before it progresses. In the same way, biblical correction addresses spiritual needs in our lives. This spiritual correction is painful, forcing us to change directions in our lives. No matter how painful, this corrective procedure protects us from future consequences that could be far more destructive. When choosing a method, you should ask, "Do I need to correct some shortcoming?"

Biblical *rebuke* works like radical surgery. The truth of Scripture confronts sin in our lives, warning us to repent or face the consequences. When choosing a method, you should ask, "Do I need to rebuke some error?"

Before you correct someone, you should rate the severity of the problem. In medicine, correct diagnosis precedes appropriate treatment. Spiritual treatment also requires correct diagnosis.

3. Apply the Method Chosen

You should apply *teaching* as your method if the person on your team needs to understand biblical truth and principles more fully. Teaching treats problems that exist and prevents future problems from erupting. As a leader, you must understand God's Word and communicate it to your team members regularly. You may teach in a formal, classroom setting. You can also teach while you work with people on a common task. You can talk about biblical principles you have learned and how they apply to that situation. Teach well. Teach often.

You should apply *instruction* as your method when you want to help your team member develop a special skill. At this stage you identify a particular problem. You work with the person until he can take appropriate action. This requires personal investment. In most cases you cannot simply teach. You must teach then work with the person until he correctly applies the principles or skills. If you instruct effectively, you can deal with problems in your team member's life before they multiply. Often people welcome instruction and sense satisfaction as they begin to use their new skills.

You should apply *correction* as your method when you must deal with a shortcoming in a team member's life. Once you detect a problem developing, you should tell the person what you have observed and why the actions concern you. Be careful to describe only what you know for sure. Describe actions; don't speculate on the motivations behind the actions. You can say, "Joe, I noticed something you did, and I was concerned for the following reasons." After your comments you can simply ask Joe if he sees this as a problem. Hopefully, Joe will agree to deal with the situation and even suggest action he could take. Together you can decide on appropriate action and agree to check progress. Correction is like spiritual surgery. Those you correct will experience some emotional pain as you confront them with something in their lives that is not right. You will have satisfaction, though, in knowing your action may save them from future pain far more severe.

You should apply *reproof* as your method when problems exist that could harm your team member and others. Reproof may be leadership's greatest challenge. Usually you will reprove only in cases of serious sin coupled with a lack of repentance. In those cases you must be sure you know the facts. You must state to the person what you know and what you have seen. You must discuss the biblical principles that apply and the consequences that will come. Depending on your team member's response, you will do all you can to urge a change of heart and a change in direction.

Reproof should break your heart. If you aren't heartbroken, you're the wrong person to reprove. Words of reproof, spoken firmly but in love, can have wonderful results. Reproof, spoken earnestly and even with tears, will often break through to a person moving toward destruction. Reproof is intensely painful for all involved. Reproof becomes love's finest hour when your team member hears and responds.

4. Nurture the Relationship

Once you have corrected a team member, you must affirm your relationship. Initially people may worry that since they have failed in a small or significant way, you may not value them as part of your team. If you had a strong relationship with them before correction, they may worry they have damaged their relationship with you. Take quick steps to reassure your team member. Invite him to work with you on some aspect of your project. Ask him to join you in a social situation where you can simply enjoy being together. Quickly he will sense that his relationship with you remains strong. In time, he can feel more secure in his relationship as he understands you corrected him because you love him.

5. Monitor the Results

Ultimately people do what you inspect, not what you expect. This leadership principle may have exceptions, but you will find it is often true. When working in correction, follow-up provides necessary accountability. Especially in higher levels of correction like reproof, accountability is essential. But at all levels, if your team members know that you will be monitoring their progress, they will take necessary steps. Once people understand that you take the correction process seriously, they will take the process seriously.

Back on the Leadership Train

If leadership is like a train, correction is basic equipment. Many leaders master the other skills: visioning, planning, enlisting, team building, communication, delegation, and motivation. The finest leaders, those who pay the price and achieve the highest results, master the skill of correction. In the end they make the greatest contribution to their vision and to those who join them to pursue that vision.

· ·

Celebration: "Doesn't That Look Great?"

· ·

HOW'S YOUR HOOPLA?

Call it celebration, recognition, affirmation, praise, or positive reinforcement. Whatever it is, best-selling authors Peters and Waterman labeled the concept "hoopla" in their classic book *In Search of Excellence*. Their study of business leadership revealed *hoopla* as a key to effectiveness, and that observation has stood the test of time. The best companies celebrate: they celebrate accomplishments, and they celebrate people.

Jesus and Celebration

Jesus understood the power of celebration. When Jesus, the ultimate leader, noticed anyone doing anything on target, He praised, affirmed, and celebrated.

Jesus saw Zacchaeus in a tree and recognized him as a man seeking God, even if only tentatively. Jesus affirmed the action by announcing in the crowd's hearing, "Zacchaeus, come down. For I must go to your house today." Celebration.

Jesus' friend Martha urged Him to command her sister Mary to leave Him and help cook supper. Jesus affirmed Mary's desire to sit at His feet and listen when He said, "Only one thing is most important, and Mary has chosen that." Celebration.

Jesus' disciple, Peter, did something unusual; he spoke profound truth. Jesus asked, "Who do people say I am?" Peter responded, "Jesus, You are the Christ, Son of the living God." Jesus affirmed Peter's response in front of all the other disciples by saying, "Flesh and blood didn't reveal this to you, Peter, but My Father who is in heaven." Celebration.

Jesus watched a poor woman drop two small coins into the collection at the temple. She followed the rich who gave money with great fanfare. Jesus affirmed her sacrificial gift before all who watched then stated, "This woman has given more than all the others." Celebration.

Jesus communicated His values, His vision, and His truth through celebration. He transferred ideas through carefully crafted words and stories. Yet He reinforced spoken truth when He celebrated truth. Jesus caught people acting on the truth taught and reinforced their action through celebration.

The Leader's Responsibility for Celebration

In their study, Peters and Waterman observed, "The institutional leader, then, is primarily an expert in the promotion and protection of values." Jesus promoted His kingdom values by celebrating, affirming, and reinforcing correct actions. Of course, He protected His values with equal force when He drove the money changers and merchants from the outer court of the temple. "My Father's house is to be a house of prayer," He cried. Yes, Jesus promoted and protected the Father's values!

If leadership is a train, celebration is the caboose. Poised at the end of the leadership process, celebration brings perspective. Celebration shapes all that precedes it. Celebration ensures that the leadership train stays on course.

Today's finest leaders celebrate the people who work with and for them. People learn what these leaders expect by what these leaders do. Team members watch their leaders closely, charting actions, noting priorities, even inconsistencies. One management consultant said, "Managers cannot really do much of value. They can only suggest what's important in the organization by what they do."

Sam Walton, founder of Wal-Mart stores, embodied this principle. Rather than staying at corporate headquarters in Arkansas, Walton visited each of his stores at least once a year. He interacted with store managers, clerks, and customers. In the early days he had only eighteen stores. By 1985, he had close to 750 stores, but still he visited each one every year. Not only that, but he often hitchhiked on Wal-Mart delivery trucks so he could visit with the drivers. He even wandered into distribution centers at 2:00 a.m. to eat doughnuts with his shift workers. Sam Walton celebrated people. People watched him. People knew his values. Sam Walton mastered the art of celebration, and that spirit of celebration began a legacy in the company that remained after his death.

Effective Christian leaders celebrate. They guide their teams and promote and protect the values of their churches, committees, or organizations through strategic celebration. They draw attention to people. As Mary Kay Ash, the founder of Mary Kay Cosmetics, said in her book *Mary Kay on People Management,* they "praise people to success."

You can become a more effective leader if you develop the art of celebration. Monitor your progress in two areas:

1. Personal celebration
2. Public celebration

Personal Celebration

Effective leaders recognize opportunities to celebrate their team members. Simple acts of thoughtfulness tell people you notice and appreciate them. Write a note, preferably handwritten. Call a team member on the phone, not to ask for anything but just to say thanks for a job well done. Catch someone doing a task and say, "I sure appreciate all you do here. I couldn't imagine this place without you."

The president of one corporation proved that it's the thought that counts when it comes to personal celebration. The company desperately needed a technical breakthrough if it were to survive. Late one evening a scientist rushed into the president's office with a working model of a new idea. The president, elated by what he saw, wanted to communicate his appreciation to the scientist. He bent forward in his chair and rummaged through his desk. He then leaned over the desk to the scientist and said, "Here." In his hand was a banana, the only reward he could immediately put his hand on. Did that count? You bet! From that time on, a small banana pin became the highest symbol of scientific achievement at this large corporation.

When it comes to personal celebration, use this maxim: Whenever you can, however you can, celebrate. Don't wait for the right moment. Don't wait for the right way. Just celebrate. Your team members will appreciate the attention and work more effectively as a result of your affirmation.

Public Celebration

Celebration becomes art when it goes public. Excellent companies from IBM to Mary Kay Cosmetics focus on public celebration to promote and protect their organization's values. IBM designed awards programs that produced many winners and celebrated the winners once they won. Mary Kay Ash built her company's marketing plan around celebrating the accomplishments of her sales consultants and directors. She said, "At Mary Kay Cosmetics, we *never* miss an opportunity to give recognition."

Do men respond to public celebration? Mary Kay Ash thought so. In *Mary Kay on People Management,* she said:

> I've often had men say to me, "Come on, now, Mary Kay, it may work for you to award ribbons, honor sales leaders on stage before large audiences, and name top achievers in your publications, but this kind of thing doesn't work with men." I just smile when I hear such remarks. Did you ever notice the stars on a six-foot seven-inch, 275-pound linebacker's helmet? Or the medals on a soldier's uniform? Men are willing to risk bodily injury and even their lives for praise and recognition!

Celebrating at Church

At our mission church in Oregon, we worked on the art of celebration. Our church anniversaries provided wonderful opportunities to celebrate our vision and values. Each year we devoted our worship service on Anniversary Sunday to celebration. We developed multimedia programs that pictured the people and places that made up our church. We invited people to share testimonies about how they came to our church and what the church meant in their lives. We had dramatic presentations that reminded us of the people who sacrificed to begin our church, making more than forty thousand long-distance phone calls from the First Baptist Church in Garland, Texas. Each year I affirmed our vision as a church and reminded our congregation of what we set out to accomplish. Then we renewed our commitment to pursue the dreams and goals God had given us. As you may imagine, Anniversary Sunday was a highlight of our year. Our children enjoyed topping off the services with birthday cake, candles, and a gymnasium full of balloons.

On another occasion we celebrated a significant missions project in our church. In January 1990, when our church was less than two years old, we sponsored our first daughter church. Since our church began through a telemarketing campaign, we continued that legacy. Most adults in our church made calls from Lake Oswego, Oregon, to Vancouver, Washington. They invited unchurched families to the new Centerpointe Church. We worked hard, laughing at the trials and tribulations of being telemarketers for Jesus.

On the Sunday morning following our phone-call blitz, we saved ten minutes at the end of our worship service for an awards ceremony. We called it the "TFJ Awards" (You guessed it: Telemarketers for Jesus Awards!). During the week I purchased some silly toys at a local toy store. My wife and I presented them to many people who made calls. We celebrated the person who made the most "dial ups" by giving the Glutton for Punishment Award. The Sneaky Snake Award went to the person who used unusual skill and persuasion to add people to our mailing list. We celebrated the person plagued with a record number of foot-in-mouth episodes with the Tongue-Tied Award. We even had fun presenting the Golden Flush Award to one of our best-natured callers who tallied the worst overall calling record. We closed our ceremony by presenting The Fantastic Phoners Award (pink and blue toy phones) to the top male and female callers. Our congregation responded throughout our ceremony with hoots, hollers, laughter, and even pride. People talked about that celebration for a long time.

We didn't do all that much; we simply took time to celebrate people. We affirmed everyone who called and everyone who tried. Most of all we said, "We value this. We want to be a church that brings others to Christ. We want to be a church that starts new churches. We did it. You did it. This is great!" And it was! When people

100

attended our church that Sunday, they had a clearer understanding of our values than ever before.

The Fine Art of Hoopla

Master the art of hoopla. Learn to celebrate. Look for excuses to celebrate. Invest the time required for public celebration. Celebrate often. Celebrate well.

Ask effective leaders, "How's your hoopla?" They may question your term, but in one way or another, they will respond, "My hoopla is great!" By their response you'll know they recognize the power of celebration and use it to direct their Leadership Train.

Are you ready for someone to ask you the same question? "How's your hoopla?" If your hoopla could be improved, improve it—starting now. As a leader, you must unleash the positive power of celebration.

The Leadership Train Model: Putting All the Pieces Together

THOSE WHO STUDY LEADERSHIP ENJOY DEBATING TOUGH
questions:

- Are leaders made, or are leaders born?
- Are leaders different from managers, and if so how?
- Is leadership about the big picture, or is leadership about the details?
- Is leadership about character or competence?
- Does leadership require grand vision or day-to-day skills?

After reading bookshelves full of books on leadership and spending more than twenty-five years in a variety of demanding leadership roles in churches and in business,

I've continued to struggle with the answers to those questions. But over time I've worried less about the abstractions of leadership and focused more and more on the hard work of leading. One thing I know for sure—after all is said and done, leadership devolves into really, really hard work. And for that hard work, leaders need practical tools they can use to think about what they must do. My quest for leadership tools led to the model presented in this book. Perhaps it will help you to see the entire model in simple chart.

The Leadership Train Model		
The Car	The Tasks	The Question
The Engine	Vision	"What do I see?"
	Personal Planning	"How do I get to what I see?"
The Passenger Car	Enlisting	"Would you like to go there with me?"
	Team Building	"How will we get there?"
The Fuel Car	Communication	"What do you see?"
	Delegation	"What's your responsibility?"
The Equipment Car	Motivation	"Why did you say 'yes'?"
	Correction	"Is something wrong here?"
The Caboose	Celebration	"Doesn't that look great?"

My view, based on years of leading, is that leaders must do all the tasks in this chart. Every leader is different. Different leaders will do particular tasks particularly well. They will also struggle with other tasks. Yet leadership is a generalist activity; specialization is just not an option. In the end, leaders must be reasonably proficient in each of the basic tasks of leadership. The good news is that these tasks require skills that can be learned and improved over time.

The challenges facing our churches, our organizations, and our world today require strong, effective leadership. We cannot settle for a handful of superleaders to get the job done. More people must step up and get involved in the process of leadership. The collective impact of a million smaller acts of leadership is the minimal requirement for our day. Some people may be "born" with unusual leadership skills, but it should not be unusual for more people to learn the skills required to lead. Leadership must become the rule and not the exception. The scope and the scale of leadership may change, but the necessity of leaders and leadership continues to mount.

Sometimes a simple model, a picture, can make a complex task easier to understand. Broken into its parts, its essential pieces, the whole of the task looks less daunting. The Leadership Train model can meet that need. Once you see the parts and grasp the whole, you can take the most important step—get started. Leaders learn by leading. Leadership is the collection of all that leaders do. To understand leadership, don't study leadership; study leaders.

When you do, you'll discover they do the tasks highlighted in the Leadership Train.

Now you know. Now lead.

Guessing the Ending

Dr. Albert Isenman, Professor of Management and Strategy at Kellogg Graduate School of Management, provided my first glimpse into the art and science of the business school case study. During the first week of the two-year MBA program, Professor Isenman began telling us the story of a tool-and-dye factory in the 1960s. He gave us background information, financial statements, and all manner of charts and graphs to help us understand the problems and challenges facing the company. He regaled us with little anecdotes about the general manager of the company and focused our attention on the dire situation. Professor Isenman scribbled on the board, asked and responded to questions, captured ideas and insights, and then sent us off to our study groups for analysis and recommendations on what the leader of the company should do in light of the problems he faced.

Individually, we read, analyzed, and made preliminary recommendations. In our study groups we debated, then agreed, and finally prepared our written recommendations. Throughout the process, we knew that this was a real company, that something had been done in the past, and the recommendation we made would be evaluated by our professor and our classmates in light of what had actually happened.

During the next class, Professor Isenman drew out of the recommendations of the various study groups. Each group had to commit to its recommendation before our classmates before we learned what had actually happened. A variety of perspectives emerged. Some groups viewed the situation as hopeless; others recommended changes that could save the company. But for that case, the predominant perspective was that the tool-and-dye company was sunk.

After further discussion, Professor Isenman asked a question with a coy smile, "So, would you like to know what actually happened?" At that point, the class would have lynched him if he had refused to disclose what he knew. And so he told us.

That was the day I started to learn the secret of the business school case study. For in the case of the tool-and-dye company, a hopeless situation with unsolvable problems was transformed into stunning success through the decisions made by the general manager. But in other cases, in future courses, companies for which the future looked bright revealed poor decision making and ended in corporate tragedy. Every case study we tackled required us to project (i.e., guess) how the story would end. Over time, I discovered that the cases that looked bleak tended to turn out well; the cases that seemed to shine with success ended up in bankruptcy. In the end, I discovered that it really didn't matter how the case ended; we learned important lessons from every case. The lessons we learned did not depend on the outcome of the case; in fact, the outcome of the case was really not the point. The leaders, the problems they faced, how they grappled with what they faced, the decisions they made with less-than-complete infor-mation—that was the point. And that is what helped us learn about leaders and leadership.

Are you wondering how the "case study" of Westside Baptist Church ended? Was it one of the hopeless cases that surprised everyone as a stunning success? Or was it one of the cases that portended success but ended up as a disap-pointment? Go ahead. Based on what you've read so far, take a guess. Then, if you'd like, I'll tell you what actually happened.

After a promising start on our first Sunday in March 1988, I spent the next five years as senior pastor of the church, working alongside two other gifted leaders, Dwight Nall and Steven Zink. We enjoyed incredible sup-port from the First Baptist Church of Garland, Texas, from the Northwest Baptist Convention, from the Interstate Baptist Association, and from the North American Mission Board. No church I know of has been given more to help it be successful. Through the next five years, God brought people to our church, people who for the most part did not have a background in church. While our church faced many struggles, I've never seen a more loving and caring group of people assembled. They gave generously of their time, money, their hearts and their lives. Whatever we lacked (and we lacked many things), the church excelled in loving service. Everyone was welcomed and loved.

Looking back, I believe the biggest mistake I made as a leader in those days was my failure to see. In my mind, I had envisioned Westside as a different type of church from the one that developed. My preconceived notion made it difficult for me to see and celebrate the church God gave us. In spite of my deficiencies, God extended grace, favor, and mercy to us. We took steps forward; we took steps backward. We had high attendance days with more than 200 in attendance; we had longer stretches with fewer than 100 in attendance and lonely summer Sundays with around 50 people in the school gym. Through the people at Westside and through those who cared about us, we had enough money to continue our ministry, but never enough not to feel financial pressure. We met in three different rented locations and moved into our fourth in 1992. During those years, people came to Christ, we developed ministries, and we learned much about worship, discipleship, and service. We even made some progress on our stated mission: "Westside is a church learning to love God and love people with creativity, passion, and joy." No period of my life has been more intense. But in no period of my life did I learn more about leadership.

When my wife, Lynn Marie, and I, along with our two daughters moved to Nashville, we left Oregon and Westside with a confusing mishmash of emotions. Our years in Oregon two thousand miles away from our families and long-time friends had cemented our marriage and our family. We discovered that God had given us each other and against all odds, as He gave us grace, we were enough. In Oregon, we developed some of the deepest friendships life offers. The joys and travails of birthing a new church drew our hearts and lives together with people in a crucible of experience that forged us. But as we began the long drive from Oregon to Tennessee, my overwhelming perspective was that I had failed. In light of all we had been given, in light of all that had been done for us by so many, I just felt guilty; I should have been able to do more as the leader.

God's grace and mercy continued for Westside. As I left, God blessed the church with a wise interim pastor to guide the church through the critical transition of moving from founding pastor to second pastor. The people of Westside rallied and God led them to a fine pastor who brought many gifts the people needed that were completely different from mine. Under his leadership, Westside continued its ministry for several more years. Ultimately, that pastor left, and Westside began its next period of change. Unfortunately, that transition proved to be too difficult and after months of noble effort, the church disbanded.

So if we consider Westside Baptist Church a business school case study, how would we describe the outcome? A success or a failure?

Ultimately, only God knows the answer to that question. But here's what I know. Most of what I know today as a leader I learned while I was at Westside. In terms of leadership, I learned far more at Westside than I did at Kellogg Graduate School of Management. In terms of spiritual leadership, Westside was God's graduate program for my life. What I did not understand at the time was that God was as interested in building me as He was in building a church. God can accomplish many things at once—start a church, expand the Kingdom, lead people to Christ, *and* give a young leader an invaluable education in spiritual leadership. Could I have been a better leader for Westside? Sure. I just could not have been a better leader without first going through the experience of Westside. Leaders learn to lead by leading. I learned at Westside.

My hope is that telling this story will encourage other leaders, not with a story of "church growth success," but with a story of God's faithfulness. I'm praying that God will help a young leader to get *on track* in leadership. I'm asking God to use this story to encourage a leader to persevere and not give up. If this story helps leaders get on track in spiritual leadership to any degree, I will be profoundly grateful to God. And so, I can now celebrate even more fully the words of the apostle Paul and boast in the Lord.

Brothers, consider your calling: not many are wise from a human perspective, not many powerful, not many of noble birth. Instead, God has chosen the world's foolish things to shame the wise, and God has chosen the world's weak things to shame the strong. God has chosen the world's insignificant and despised things—the things viewed as nothing—so He might bring to nothing the things that are viewed as something, so that no one can boast in His presence. But from Him you are in Christ Jesus, who for us became wisdom from God, as well as righteousness, sanctification, and redemption, in order that, as it is written: The one who boasts must boast in the Lord. (1 Cor 1:26–31)